Put Beginning Readers on the Right Track with
ALL ABOARD READING™

The All Aboard Reading series is especially designed for beginning readers. Written by noted authors and illustrated in full color, these are books that children really want to read—books to excite their imagination, expand their interests, make them laugh, and support their feelings. With fiction and nonfiction stories that are high interest and curriculum-related, All Aboard Reading books offer something for every young reader. And with four different reading levels, the All Aboard Reading series lets you choose which books are most appropriate for your children and their growing abilities.

Picture Readers
Picture Readers have super-simple texts, with many nouns appearing as rebus pictures. At the end of each book are 24 flash cards—on one side is a rebus picture; on the other side is the written-out word.

Station Stop 1
Station Stop 1 books are best for children who have just begun to read. Simple words and big type make these early reading experiences more comfortable. Picture clues help children to figure out the words on the page. Lots of repetition throughout the text helps children to predict the next word or phrase—an essential step in developing word recognition.

Station Stop 2
Station Stop 2 books are written specifically for children who are reading with help. Short sentences make it easier for early readers to understand what they are reading. Simple plots and simple dialogue help children with reading comprehension.

Station Stop 3
Station Stop 3 books are perfect for children who are reading alone. With longer text and harder words, these books appeal to children who have mastered basic reading skills. More complex stories captivate children who are ready for more challenging books.

In addition to All Aboard Reading books, look for All Aboard Math Readers™ (fiction stories that teach math concepts children are learning in school); All Aboard Science Readers™ (nonfiction books that explore the most fascinating science topics in age-appropriate language); and All Aboard Poetry Readers™ (funny, rhyming poems for readers of all levels).

All Aboard for happy reading!

For Kyle, Stephen, and Amy—J.D.

To Anthony and Adriel—P.J.

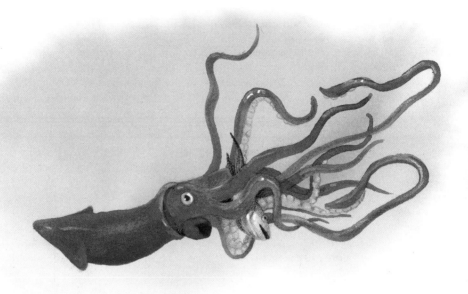

Photo credits: AMNH/Portia Rollings.

Thanks are given to Dr. Neil H. Landman, Dr. Paula Mikkelsen, Dr. Steve O'Shea, and all of the AMNH Squid Team.

Published by Grosset & Dunlap, a division of Penguin Young Readers Group, 345 Hudson Street, New York, NY 10014. GROSSET & DUNLAP and ALL ABOARD SCIENCE READER are trademarks of Penguin Group (USA) Inc. Printed in the U.S.A.

Library of Congress Cataloging-in-Publication Data

Dussling, Jennifer.
    Giant squid : mystery of the deep / by Jennifer Dussling ; illustrated by Pamela Johnson.
    p.   cm. — (All aboard reading. Level 2)
    Summary: Describes a giant squid recently found off the coast of New Zealand, whose twenty-five-foot-long body can now be studied by scientists to reveal more facts about this mysterious creature of the deep.
    1. Giant squids—Juvenile literature. [1. Giant squids. 2. Squids.] I. Johnson, Pamela, ill. II. Title. III. Series.
QL430.3.A73D87   1999
594'.58—dc21

ISBN   0-448-41995-5   I J

American Museum
of Natural History

GIANT SQUID

Mystery of the Deep

By Jennifer Dussling
Illustrated by Pamela Johnson

Grosset & Dunlap • New York

Chapter 1

December 1997

Far away, off the coast of New Zealand,

a fishing boat floats on the ocean waves.

It's a large boat,

and it will stay out at sea

for many months.

The crew drops big nets way down deep.

This helps them catch more fish.

Then they pull in the nets.

Today they get a big surprise.

In one of the nets

there is something dark red and long—

about 25 feet long.

It's no fish.

That's for sure.

The fishermen know what it is.

It is a dead giant squid—

one of the most mysterious creatures

in the world!

They also know there's one man

who will be very happy

to hear about this.

But he will have to wait.

They still have many weeks of fishing.

Chapter 2

Venice, Italy

March 1998

Three months later

Neil Landman gets a call.

Neil works for the American Museum

of Natural History in New York City.

He's an expert on squids.

But it is late at night.

And he's on vacation in Italy.

Who would call him now?

It's a friend from New Zealand.

His friend is also a squid expert.

"We have a giant squid," he says to Neil.

"Do you want it?"

Neil can't believe it.

A giant squid!

He has hoped and hoped for years

to have one for the museum.

Of course he wants it!

It is no wonder Neil is so excited.

The giant squid is a great mystery.

It lives deep in the ocean,

nearly a mile below the surface.

There are no giant squids in zoos.

No one has ever caught one alive.

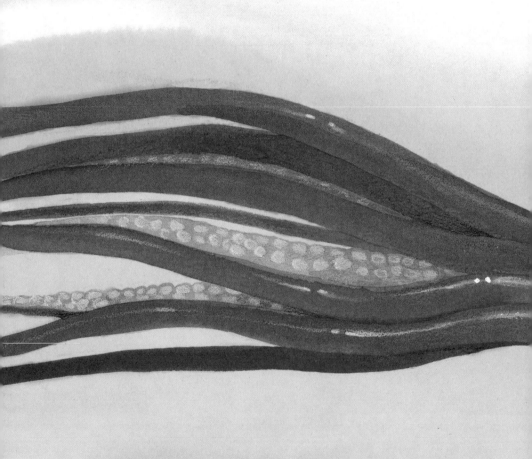

So not much is known
about these creatures.
We don't know for sure
how long they live,
how quickly they grow,
how fast they swim,
or whether they live together
or alone.

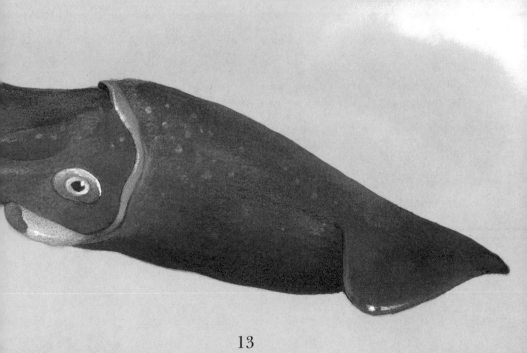

Every once in a while,
part of a dead giant squid
will wash up on a beach.

But usually people find

just a long tentacle or two.

Long ago,

people thought these tentacles

had to belong to a huge monster.

They told stories

about a monster

called the kraken.

With its long arms and giant suckers,

the kraken grabbed ships.

It pulled them under the water.

It ate all the sailors.

Today we know

there are no krakens.

There are giant squids,

but they are not monsters.

We know they don't attack people.

A giant squid is just like

a regular squid—

but much bigger!

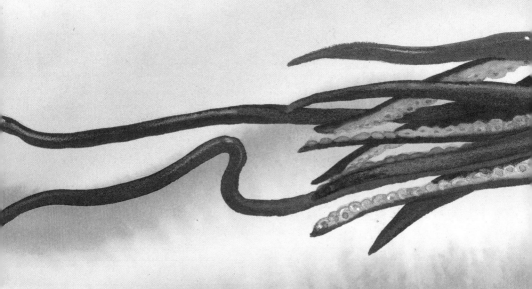

A squid is usually less than 1 foot long.

A giant squid can grow

up to 60 feet long!

A giant squid also has the biggest eyes

of any animal.

Its eyes can be as big as soccer balls!

The giant squid has a short body
called a mantle.
This is where its brain
and eyes and mouth are.
But most of the squid's length
comes from its eight arms
and two long feeding tentacles.

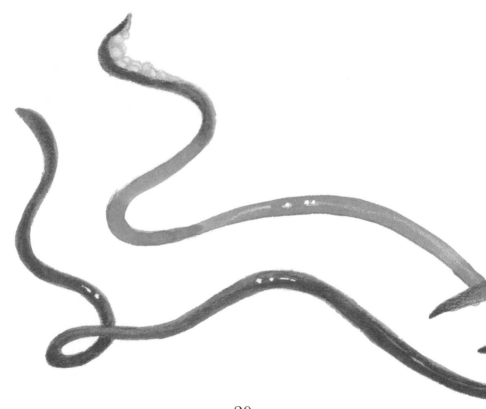

21

Water goes in through the mantle.

The squid is a smooth swimmer.

It does not need its arms to swim,

the way you do.

Instead, the squid sucks

water into its mantle.

Then it tightens the muscles in its body

to force the water out the funnel.

Water is squeezed out
through the funnel.

This pushes the squid forward!

Small fins on the side of its body

help the squid to steer.

It shoots through the water like a bullet.

Squids are cousins to the octopus.
Everyone knows an octopus has
eight arms just like a squid.
But an octopus does not have
the two extra-long feeding tentacles.
Squids and octopi both belong to a
group of animals called <u>cephalopods</u>
(you say it like this: SEF-a-lo-podz).

Cephalopods are strong and smart and fast.

They have no bones in their bodies.

They can squeeze into small spaces.

There they hide and wait for food.

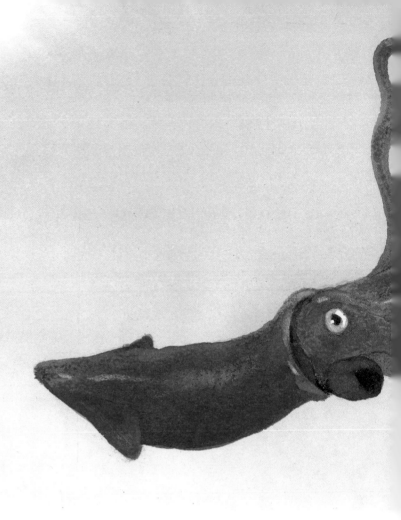

The giant squid's body is perfect

for catching other animals.

Rows of suckers line its arms.

Each sucker has a ring of sharp teeth.

The giant squid is fierce.

It grabs a fish with its arms.

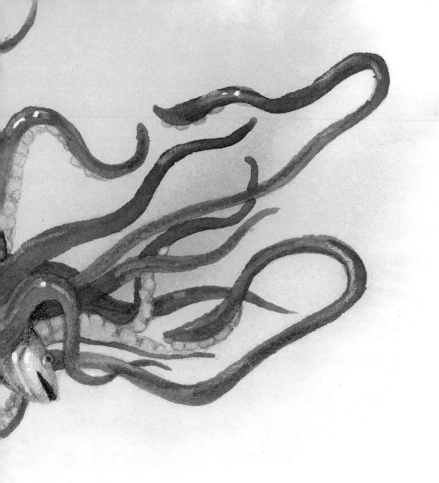

The toothed suckers sink into the skin.

The fish cannot get away.

Then the squid drags the fish

to its mouth.

Besides fish, giant squids also eat

smaller squids and shrimp.

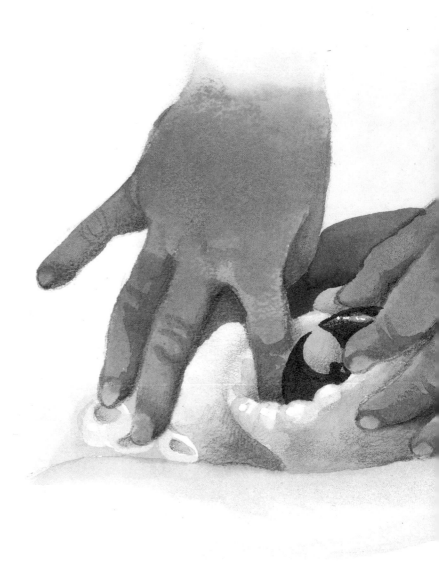

Like other cephalopods,

the giant squid has a beak in its mouth.

A beak?

Yes!

This beak is a lot like a bird's beak.

It is very sharp.

A giant squid's beak can bite through

the steel cable of a ship!

The giant squid has only one real enemy:

the sperm whale.

Far below the ocean waves,

sperm whales battle giant squids.

How do we know?

Giant squid beaks are often found
in the bellies of sperm whales.
And the skin of the sperm whales
shows that the squid put up a fight.
The squid's suckers leave
lots of scars on the whale.
But no one has ever seen a battle
between these two mighty creatures.

There are many things

we do not know about giant squids.

Some smaller squids

can change their color

to blend in with rocks or coral.

Can giant squids do that?

We don't know.

Other squids glow in the dark.

Do giant squids?

We don't know.

Some cephalopods squirt out ink
to confuse an enemy.
Can giant squids squirt ink?
Maybe.
Maybe not.
It's still a mystery.

Chapter 3

New York City—June 1998

Neil Landman wants to solve

some of the mysteries of the giant squid.

But most of all

he wants to see his squid.

He paces back and forth

in the airport waiting room.

His whole staff paces

back and forth with him.

The squid arrives in a huge plastic case.

It is frozen solid.

That's how the fishermen

kept it so long!

A truck takes the squid to the museum.

Now the interesting work can begin!

Neil starts to defrost it.

He injects it with

a chemical that will keep it fresh.

It is a strong chemical.

It is not healthy to breathe it in.

Neil and his helpers have to wear masks.

Two weeks later

they wash the squid with water.

It is kept in a big tank.

They refill the tank

with alcohol.

Then the real work begins.

Neil measures the squid.

He weighs it.

He examines it

from the top of its mantle

to the tip

of its tentacles.

The museum takes pictures.

The scientists will learn a lot
from this squid.
Already Neil has found out
something interesting.
The squid weighs only 200 pounds
and is 25 feet long.
At first people thought it was a baby.
But it is not a baby at all!
It is a full-grown male squid.

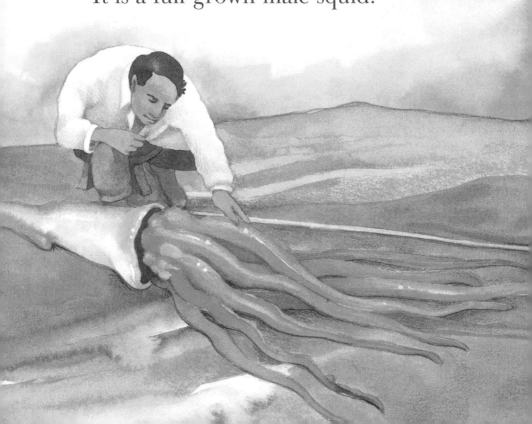

Most of the giant squids
that scientists had seen before
were female.
Neil's squid is the first full-grown male.
This means female squids
are much bigger than males.

Neil cuts out the squid's beak.

He puts it in a jar.

It is beautiful.

It looks almost like a shell,

brown and yellow.

But why did he cut it out?

Now he can learn more about

how the beak works.

And he wants to be able

to show it to people.

It was hard to see

when it was inside the squid.

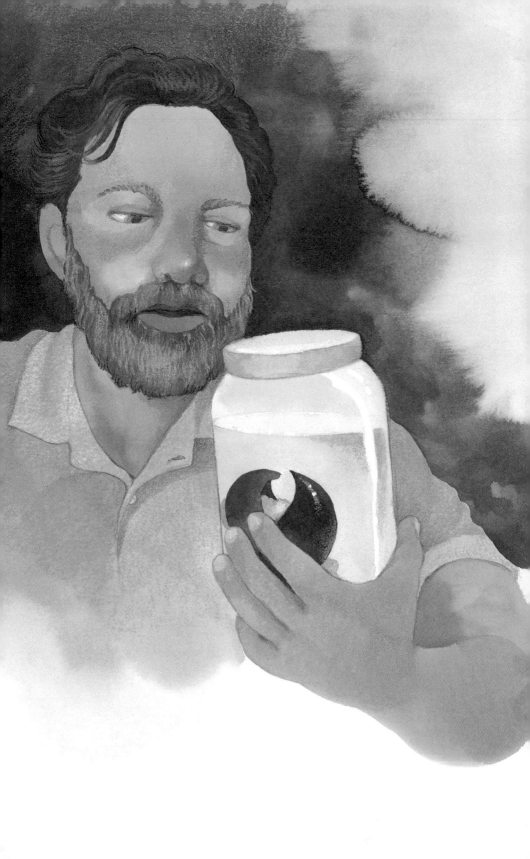

Lots of people want to see Neil's squid.

People who work in the museum.

Squid experts.

Students who are studying cephalopods.

So Neil sets up times

to show off the squid.

The giant steel tank is wheeled out.

The lid is taken off.

Everyone steps back at first.

The smell is very strong.

But then the people crowd in to look.

It is an incredible sight.

The squid is famous.

Reporters write articles about it

in newspapers.

There is something about giant squids

that interests everyone.

Right now only a few people
can see the squid.
But Neil hopes that soon
hundreds of people
will be able to see it every day.
He hopes that the squid will be
put on display
in the museum.

Then kids from all over

could learn more about

this great mystery of the deep.